Smart Story *for* Smart Learner

SMART STORY
for
Smart Learner

Learn popular phrases, idioms and proverbs while enjoying the story!

•

Nitin Sharma

Illustrations
Sumit & Sonal

F-2/16, Ansari Road, Daryaganj, New Delhi-110002
E-mail: info@unicornbooks.in • *Website:* www.unicornbooks.in

Branch : Mumbai
23-25, Zaoba Wadi Thakurdwar, Mumbai-401002
☎ 022-22010941, 022-22053387
E-mail: rapidex@bom5.vsnl.net.in

Showroom :
★ **PM Publications,** New Delhi
- 10-B, Netaji Subhash Marg, Daryaganj
  New Delhi-110002
- 6686, Khari Baoli, Delhi-110006

ISBN: 978-81-7806-305-8

Edition: 2012

Printed at : *Unique Color Carton, Mayapuri, New Delhi-110064*

To Those
Who Try Innovative Ways to
Combine Study With Fun

A Word From the Author

Hello friends,

English is, undoubtedly, the true global language. This wonderful language has been enriched by a number of popular sayings. 'SMART STORY: FOR SMART LEARNER' encompasses more than one hundred and fifty carefully chosen proverbs, idioms and phrases. The knowledge of English is incomplete without understanding them. This book is an attempt to teach how to use them while writing or speaking. They have been provided in italics for your convenience. So, enjoy the story, and master the language. I'm sure you will find this innovative way of learning English more interesting than the traditional way of mugging up words and phrases. And remember, your brain remembers stories better than information.

Happy reading!

How To Use This Book

The meanings of proverbs, idioms and phrases used in the story have been provided in the last few pages of the book. Whenever you confront a difficult phrase, all you need to do is turn the pages and look for the meaning. It's that easy! I suggest you read the story more than once to get well acquainted with them.

Happy reading!

Contents

The 'Lion' of All Troubles

"Wonder Forest" is a heaven on earth. It is a small, strikingly beautiful, green forest island in the lap of a big river, and merely touches the land by a narrow passage. All the animals living on this *awe inspiring* island are friends. They live in perfect harmony. If you ever visit Wonder Forest, you will find them playing, chatting, singing, dancing or partying together. But, ALAS!… this day was an exception. It indeed was. They were discussing a grave matter, after all. Actually, the fate of the island was *in the melting pot*! We *gave an ear* to their conversation.

Bobby, the bear, couldn't believe the horrible news at once. "My, my, my! Are you hundred percent sure they are coming towards us, Eggie?"

"*Seeing is believing*, buddy," said Eggie the eagle, nodding his head. "They were thrown out by an enemy *pride*. Now they have only two options — either cross the river or occupy our beloved home, our island. And they wouldn't risk their lives trying to cross an overflowing river."

"*Misfortune never comes alone,* I guess," said Chimp, the chimpanzee. "A river overflowing in winter? Who could have imagined? Could be because of men's activities... By the way, how many lions, Eggie?"

"Five killer cats. All brothers."

"How do you know they're brothers?"

"They were calling each other 'brother'."

Zebby, the little Zebra, was *scared stiff*. Finally, he gathered courage and spoke, "Boy, lions love to eat zebras! We must run far, far away *as soon as possible*. I'll inform my parents about them, and by evening, we shall..."

"Don't be *chicken-hearted*, 'Mr. quick'." Oxy, the brave little ox, who found his response cowardly, interrupted him and offered an unsought advice. "We can't give up so easily. We should *fight tooth and nail* for our home."

'*Empty vessels make the most noise*, 'Mr. brave'. What do you know about lions?" teased Zebby questioned his wisdom.

Monk, the old monkey, paid no attention to the kids' arguments. He looked to the sky and prayed, "Holy God! Almighty! Protect us. Why are you sending the lions?"

Horsy, the young horse, the naughtiest kid in the forest, was absorbed in his own world. Suddenly, he turned his head and asked Bobby, "Hey Uncle Bobby, is it true that lions demand *'lion's share'* in everything, because they are the lions?"

"How smart!" said Zebby, with sarcasm in his tone. But Jeffry, the old Giraffe, agreed with Horsy. He looked at Bobby and nodded. (Giraffes can't speak.)

Bobby knew his answer would lead to another question, so he ignored Horsy's question and turned to Rhiny, "Will you guide us, Rhiny my friend?"

Rhiny, the rhino, was an aged and strong animal. "Bobby, *to be honest*, I'm not worried about myself, as lions won't dare challenge a rhino. But I'm worried about you guys." He looked at everyone. "You are my family. I promise I'll help you *heart and soul* if there's a battle. However, I'd prefer to avoid a battle with them. I suggest we should try to keep the lions away from this island. Once they enter, it won't be easy to drive them out. They are *born killers*. Let's *nip the danger in the bud*."

Moly, the Mole, had the same opinion. "Yeah… It's like *'win the horse or lose the saddle'* for us. Either we keep our home, or we lose everything we have… may be our lives!"

Little Horsy didn't quite understand what was said, "Hey Uncle Moly, did you say something like 'win the horse…' "

"It's not about you, naughty boy," clarified Moly. Then he turned to Eggie, "Hey Ego, what do you think, how long will they take?"

"Four days or less, depending on their pace.

One of them has got a broken leg, so he can't walk fast."

"I'm afraid that won't help much. We are running out of time, fellow... Let's go and meet Elphy. He had once lived near the lions. His experience can save us," said Bobby, with a sense of urgency. "And we better hurry. *A stitch in time saves nine.*"

Elphy was a big elephant, a nice giant. He lived near the river. All the animals rushed to his place. To their surprise, they found him sleeping under a Banyan tree.

Horsy couldn't hide his astonishment. "Do you see him, Uncle? He is *as mute as a fish*, *as free as air*, and as lazy as himself. He is always *in smooth waters*, no matter how bad the situation is."

This time he qualified for a scolding. And Bobby did just that, "Shut up, you little fellow. You must respect the elders. Even though he's friendly with kids, he is fifteen years older than you. *Think before you speak.*"

Elphy *took them by surprise*, "And guys, I'm *a light sleeper*. Even the whispers wake me up. And you guys were so loud that you could wake a dead… Eh… let's *bury the hatchet.* Tell me, what brings you guys here? Something serious?"

"*Dead serious*, my friend," said Eggie. "We are in *grave danger*."

"Why… What's the matter? Has anyone seen a man with a gun?"

Bobby explained the matter, "No, Elphy. We don't know what a 'gun' is, but it's not about that. A pride of lions is headed towards our island. Once they reach here, it will be all *'might is right'* situation. You know them. They are the kings of the jungle, and *'kings can do no wrong'*."

"Oops! The big cats? I guess you are right. It's worse than a man with a gun. Lions are too fierce to befriend. So… I suppose you guys have a plan?"

"Not so far. We thought you would suggest something," said Chimp.

"Hmmm… No doubt, I understand their ways… Let me think… hmmm… peaceful ones against fierce ones… doesn't sound good… Guys, the first thing we all need to realize is that *union is strength.* Let it be understood that *we shall sink or swim together.* And we have very few options. Either run away, or face the lions."

"Face the lions?" Little Horsy was surprised to hear the latter option. "Uncle, do you think that's an option? That is a *sure shot* way of committing suicide."

Gurela, the young Gorilla, an angry chap, felt compelled to say something, "Uncle, I don't wanna leave this island. I'm a fighter, and this is my home. I believe in *taking the bull by the horns.*"

"Oh please Gurela, *don't build castles in the air.* You know lions are mighty. We can't take them *head-on.*" Zebby didn't want anyone to say anything about battle or fight.

"Look cry baby, I know only one rule-- '*Fortune favours the brave*'. So, please don't teach me…"

"Enough, kids," Bobby had to intervene, "No quarrel, please. Let the elders talk."

"Uncle, he started it," complained Gurela.

"Yes. But *it takes two to quarrel.* Now, let's get

back on track. What would you say, Elphy? Should we fight? Or should we leave the island?"

"I think our 'Zebby-debby' is right. It will be a *'mare's nest'* to assume that we can beat lions in a direct fight." Elphy took a deep breath, and thought for a moment. "Hmmm... Before we *arrive at a decision*, we must consult Aunty Katy. She can definitely guide us. Cats are the aunts of big cats, after all."

Katy was a wise old cat. Although the cats are known to be opportunistic animals, this one was not. She used to live in a cave and spend her time remembering God and taking care of children when the elders were busy gathering food. Katy had no children of her own, so she treated them as her own children. All the animals respected her. And she loved everyone.

The animals headed for Katy's cave.

Katy Gives the Idea

Aunt Katy already knew about the coming trouble, "Oh yes… I got the news, children. In fact, we should have foreseen the trouble. *Coming events cast their shadows before.* Most of the monkeys in the neighbourhood have already left their island. The vultures have gathered near the old dunes. They feed on whatever the lions abandon. All these were early warning signs for us. After all, there is *no smoke without fire.*"

"Katy, tell us. Should we fight or should we leave the place, as our neighbours did?" asked Bobby.

"Bobby, if we leave this island, we may not

find another safe place to live. The lions, the tigers, the wolves and the hyenas rule the jungle. We have been very lucky to have this island as our home."

Deery, a fawn (baby deer), whispered softly, "But Aunty, if we stay, we will have to fight the lions. And I don't think we can beat them."

Katy smiled at him and said, "True, my child. We can't defeat them by muscle. But, your mind is mightier than the muscle and deeper than the sea. But, who said we have to fight them? After all, there is no *bad blood* between us and them. We should find a way to change their direction."

"But Aunty, they can go nowhere else. The overflowing river is blocking their path to the next jungle. They wouldn't risk their lives, would they?" Chimp reminded her.

"Well, in that case, you should help them cross the river. They will cross the river and we will retain our home. That will be *a win-win situation*," replied clever Katy. "And children, you must plan your defenses *as soon as possible*, just in case the things go out of control. *Help your luck, so that your luck helps you*. Remember, *God helps those who help themselves*."

"But Aunty, how do we make them cross the river?" asked Elphy.

"That's pretty simple. They will cross the river if they find a nice bridge spanning it."

"Ohh... well, perhaps we can do that," he looked at Elphy, who nodded. "But what if they still come towards us?"

"Well, provide them a good reason to stay away from this island. Either scare them away, or lure them to the huge neighbouring jungle. Do either and you will keep your home."

"I think we must do both. We should *leave no stone unturned*," suggested Bobby.

"And how would we know what scares them and what interests them?" questioned Moly.

"I know. I had been kept in a circus before I *broke free*. Men use fire and guns to keep the lions under control. Fire scares the lions. And I know how to create fire." Elphy told them with a sense of pride.

"And food, like myself, lures them," Zebby added innocently.

"Don't forget folks, fire can burn us too. It's *a double-edged sword*," cautioned Chimp.

"Don't worry, Chimp. I'll take care of that," assured Elphy. "We will use river water in case we need to extinguish the fire. I can use my long trunk to throw water on it."

"Good idea, son. Let the lions know it would be better not to enter this island. And they will not come. God bless you, children. I'll pray for your success," said Aunt Katy.

All the animals left the cave and reached their official meeting place: a rock under a centuries-old Banyan tree.

Here's the Plan

Bobby called a meeting of all the animals of Wonder Forest. Parro (the parrot), the messenger of animals, had already informed them about the coming danger and how Bobby had planned to face it. Everyone respected Bobby for his wisdom and sincerity, so no one objected to the plan. When they gathered near the tree, Bobby spoke to them, "Friends! Lions are not too far from here. We have to oppose them *might and main*. I hope you all know the plan. And since you have no objections, let's make preparations for fire, and let's construct a bridge. Parents will build defenses around their shelters so that children could hide, just in case our plan seems to fail.

Anyone who is free shall help us. I doubt if fire alone would be able to keep the lions away. So we'll plan some more tricks. Any suggestions are most welcome."

Mr. Bull spoke on behalf of parents, "Bobby, we all admire your insight and dedication. Please go ahead with your plan. We'll do as you say."

Bobby felt empowered as he heard these words. "Thank you for your trust, friends. I won't disappoint you. Let's begin then, shall we?"

"Eggie, you must *keep an eye on* the lions," advised Moly. "We must *know which way the wind blows.*"

"*Rest assured,* fellows. They can't escape my sharp vision. I'll start my work right away." Punctual Eggie left immediately. Anxious parents got busy covering their shelters with small rocks, thorns, and tree branches.

Bobby distributed the work among the rest of them, "Elphy, you are *in command* of our defence team. You have to build a temporary bridge over the river. We will push it into the river as soon as the lions cross it. Chimp, you have to collect wood and dry leaves for fire. And Moly, I have a special task for you. Your friends and you have to dig a small, wide ditch near the main passage to discourage the lions from entering. We will fill it with water. This is another part of our plan. We want to create as many hurdles as possible. And remember, we have three days or less. So, please hurry up my friend. Remember, *time and tide wait for none.*"

"Can we really make all this happen, Uncle Bobby?" Horsy asked eagerly, as he was not quite convinced.

"Kid, I know it's a *Herculean task*, but if we work as a team, we can. Impossible says I-M-POSSIBLE."

Let There Be a Bridge

Elphy built a team of strong, muscular animals--rhino, bull, horse and others. They were supposed to construct a bridge on the river. It was no *child's play*. Lions are heavy animals. The bridge had to be strong enough to support their massive bodies; or else they wouldn't cross it. At the same time, the bridge had to be light enough so that the animals could push it into the river whenever they desired.

Elphy stopped near a tree. He observed it for a while. "Hmmm… Friends, I want a collection of three strong 'Shisham' logs near the river bank by this evening. This one looks good. Let's bring it down…"

"No Elphy," objected Monk. "We should not destroy any green trees. There are many dried ones in the Western part of our island. Use them for the bridge."

Boary, the boar, didn't *share the same opinion.* So he queried, "But Monk, isn't the Western part a bit far from here? Why take so much trouble?"

"It's not very far from here. And don't forget, my friend, *life is precious.* Trees are our Gods. They provide us food, fresh air and shelter. If you destroy nature, the nature will destroy you. It's always '*tit for tat*'."

Little Horsy agreed with him, "Mr. Monk is right. My teacher says we should protect the jungle. And we still have sufficient time, Uncle. We can work together and take the tree trunks to the river bank."

"Dear Horsy, what a wise kid you are!" Boary patted him on the back.

They all agreed to spare the green trees and walked to the Western part of the island. This part had *bore the brunt* of forest fire last year.

As soon as they reached there, Chimp started his job, "Let me find the suitable ones." He climbed up a tall tree and spotted three dead tree trunks *in no time.*

"And I'll pull them down for you." Elphy loosened up his body for the strenuous task.

"We'll help you, Uncle Elphy." little Zebby was eager to see how a massive tree is brought down, and he also wanted to be a part of this process.

But Horsy wanted to avoid the hard work. "Uncle, it will be *a hard nut to crack* to carry these huge ones. Can't we choose the smaller ones instead?"

"*No pleasure without pain*, Horsy dear. You are jungle kids. You MUST be tough. Besides, *if a job is worth doing, it is worth doing well*.... All right fellows! Let's begin," ordered Elphy.

Elphy pulled the nearest of the three trees with full might, using his long trunk. Boary, Rhiny, Horsy, and Zebby pushed the tree from the other side. They had to try *once and again*, as the deep roots of tree held the soil firmly. Finally, the huge dead tree was brought down. One by one they brought down all the three dried trunks. It took them hours to finish the task. By the evening, they were *dead on their feet.* Though they were behind the set schedule, yet they decided to *call it a day.*

Elphy was tired but vigilant. "Hey, where is Olu (*the owl*)? We can send him to see how the work is going in Moly's team. How much have they done *so far*?"

Parro gave their message to Olu. Soon Olu reached the site. He was a delightful creature, with not a very good sense of humor. Teasing Moly was his favourite profession.

"Hi friends! What a beautiful morning it is, isn't it?"

"Morning? It's night, Uncle Olu," Horsy corrected him.

"That's why we need him, kid. Our night is his morning. He can see clearly in the dark. Hey Olu, could you do us a favour, please? Go and see if Moly and team have begun their job," said Chimp.

"*By all means,* buddy. I'd love to disturb him. Wu hu hu hu huu..." And Olu took off right away.

Moly had organized a team of moles and rats. They were expert at digging. What the strong, muscular animals couldn't do, these small creatures could. After all, *size doesn't matter.*

Olu reached the place where Moly and friends were trying to take rest after a lot of hard work.

"Hellooooooow Moly, my friend!" Olu said in a lighter vein.

"Hey! Could you please stop shouting? Can't you see we are trying to sleep?" said Moly, as he got irritated.

"Chimp sent me to check the progress of work. I thought I should have a little chat with you before I leave."

"Stop kidding, guy. We are extremely tired."

"Let me sing you a lullaby then. Shall I?"

"All right, funny. Do what you want. *Every dog has its day*. Likewise every owl has its night. We will see you tomorrow morning when you will be trying to sleep. I'll make sure you have a tough sleep."

Olu laughed his heart out, "Wuuu hu hu hu hu huuu… Hey, I was just kidding pal ... *Take it easy*. I leave you in peace my sweet Moly-goly. Sweet dreams!"

Olu left the place without causing any more disturbance. He muttered to himself, "He is pretending as if his heart is *as hard as a flint*, and he is *as hoarse as a crow*. But I know he is a Mr. nice. Perhaps he is *having a tough time* digging the ditch." Soon he reached where Elphy and his team were resting.

"Welcome back, Olu- golu. So…what's the good news?" Chimp asked cheerfully.

"The good news is that they are trying their level best. And the bad news is that I don't think they can dig deep enough in three days. They are too few *to make it in time*."

"I had *figured that out* even before they started." Elphy didn't look bothered at all.

"Then why didn't you tell them, uncle?" asked Horsy.

Elphy replied, "Because I have *a fool proof plan,* kid. Even if they *miss the target*, I'll *make up for* it. Let them do their best. May be they can *do the impossible*. Why discourage them?"

"Good thinking, Elphy. I hope they do succeed. And kids, don't forget *there is no hard and fast way to success*. Even we will have *to burn the candle at both ends* from tomorrow onwards. Let's preserve our energy. Good night everyone!" wished Chimp.

"Good night!" they wished each other. But Olu didn't. "Good morning guys! Have a nice sleep," he said.

A sound sleep indeed recharged them to perform the *mammoth task* of transporting the logs to the river bank. Next morning, they woke up refreshed. After a quick breakfast, they started again.

Elphy picked up one log in his trunk. "I'll take this one with me. You guys have to carry the rest of them. Then, we will plan our next move."

"Uncle, is it not too heavy for you?" asked Zebby.

"I'll manage, kid."

Moving a huge log was not too tough a task for Elphy, as he had a well-built body and a long trunk. But, it was for everyone else, even for Rhiny, as the rhinos have no trunks to lift something.

The size of the log worried the kids. Horsy asked Chimp, "Uncle, how do we *move the mountain*? The log is *too heavy to lift*."

Chimp came up with a solution, "Don't lift it. Just push. Everyone, come here! *Throw a team together*. We will work *in a body*, and will take one log at a time. Kids, it's the best opportunity for you to realise the importance of team-work."

Oxy, Horsy, Zebby and Rhiny came together and stood behind the log. Other comrades began to clear the path. As Chimp counted "a three…a two… a one… and GO", they pushed the log. The trick worked! They were successfully pushing the heavy log despite the friction of uneven land. But, after pushing the log about half a kilometer, the kids were *out of breath*.

"Come on kids! We have to *keep the things rolling*. We haven't covered even one-third of the distance. HIP HIP HURRAY!" Boary wanted to motivate them. But, he didn't receive the expected response.

"Huff…huff… Let's stop Uncle Boary… and take a breath. Huff… I'm *dog tired*," said Horsy.

"That's because you are *putting the cart before the horse*, kid. You should move your forelegs first. Instead, you are pushing the ground with your hind legs."

Zebby was *second to none* in making excuses. "I think I have got a sprain in my right leg."

"You always have an excuse. You should be *as brave as a lion*, because we have to face the lions," complained Horsy.

"Huh…*Only the wearer knows where the shoe pinches*. And what are YOU doing?" grumbled Zebby.

"I knew you were a cry baby…"

"All right…all right… *Don't make much ado about nothing*." Chimp examined his legs. "Nothing wrong, kid. Take a ten-minute break and move on. No excuses."

Soon they started again. After moving the log for about two hours, they were near the river. Elphy was waiting for them. He was shocked to see that they carried only one log with them. "Only one log? I thought you would *knock off* by the evening."

"Sir, it's easy for you to give orders. But you don't realize what we *went through* to get the log here," replied exhausted Zebby. Other kids nodded.

Elphy realized his mistake, "Ok, ok... Cool down, kids. My mistake. I thought you would get some help. I'll bring the last one. You guys take care of the two lying here." And he left for the third log.

Zebby noticed something unusual. "Hey, do you see that? There are three crocs lying near the river bank. Should we tell them to go away?"

"Shhhh... *Let sleeping dogs lie*. Crocs are dangerous. They won't listen to us. Don't bother them," cautioned Chimp.

"My God, the river is flowing much above its level! Will our bridge be stable here?" Boary looked concerned.

"Not here," answered Chimp. "We will have to *hang around* and *find a weak spot* in the flow. That is where our bridge will be set up. Let Elphy, Bobby and other friends reach here."

In the evening, Elphy arrived with the third log. Bobby had called for a second meeting of all the animals, so that they could see the progress of work. After all, it was important to get their wholehearted support. They all gathered at the proposed site. Jacky, the jackal, also reached there, even though he was not seen around since months.

"I'm quite *at sixes and sevens* if we should allow Jacky to attend the meeting. He has always been *a black sheep*. He *plays fast and loose*," said Chimp.

"I know he is not *a man of words*. But, even his family lives on this island. He won't deceive us this time. Besides, he apologized in public when he was caught *red handed* stealing the food from the 'reserve cave'. Let's give him a chance," opined Bobby.

Bobby now addressed the animals. "Friends, as you all know, a grave crisis is *staring us in the face*. And we had taken a *unanimous decision* that we'd fight for our home. Though it may seem difficult *to tide over the crisis*, but believe me, if we work together, we can win. I have seen many *ups and downs* in my life. And my experience says this crisis is no bigger than a forest fire or a flood. We must stand united for our home....We will not let the lions enter our island. We will *show them fight*. And I'm sure we shall win. ARE YOU WITH ME?"

All the animals shouted in one voice "Yesss! WE SHALL WIN… WE SHALL WIN… WE SHALL WIN." The encouraging words had filled every heart with enthusiasm. They were now ready to challenge the lions, the undisputed kings of the jungle.

"Great! Then be prepared for a glorious victory. Our *slow but sure* progress will lead us to success," assured Bobby.

Suddenly, Eggie arrived with the latest, "Bobby, lions are just a few miles away! They are faster than we thought. They will be here in a day. Right now they are feeding on the only old deer left in the neighbourhood. There were some bear cubs and colts left behind. I've told them to join our protection. They will be here *in a while*."

"Good job, Eggie. It's our duty to help those innocent kids. After all, *a friend in need is a friend indeed*," said Bobby.

Gurela was angry, very angry, and very eager to meet the lions. He had no fear at all. "I'm waiting for the big cats. *The sooner, the better.* Let them see whom they intend to mess with."

And this challenge started a chain reaction among the kids. All the kids started *to blow their own trumpets.*

"I'll take two of them…" said Oxy.

"They will see how good my kicks are..." added Horsy.

"All right bravos. Let's finish our job first," Elphy needed to remind them. Then he looked at Moly, who looked a bit discouraged. "Moly, you look tired and upset!"

"My friend, I'm afraid we won't be able to *make it* by tomorrow… We tried our best, but the soil is a bit hard and rocky in this part of the island."

"I appreciate your efforts, pal. I heard you people are *burning the midnight oil.* Yet it is not easy to dig a ditch in this hard soil. Don't worry. My *contingency plan* is ready. We will surround it with big sharp thorns. On the other side will be our fire. They won't even dare look this side," said Elphy.

"And if they still don't leave?" Zebby was still not fully convinced.

Elphy wanted to have a little fun. "Hmmm… In that case, we will hand a little zebra over to them. They will spare us." He laughed out loud as he said these words, "A-HA-HA-ha-ha-ha-hah…".

Zebby was frightened. "Whattt? Look uncle Bobby…he says… he says…"

Bobby patted him on his back gently, "Calm down, Zebby dear. He is just teasing you. Be brave. And you Elphy… Don't scare the kids. Grow up now."

"Sorrrrrry… sorry kid. It was a joke. Won't happen again." Elphy touched his ear.

"A bad joke," frowned Zebby.

Aunt Katy was full of hope, but she was *down to earth* too. "*God's will be done*. But we must *hope for the best and prepare for the worst*."

"Don't worry Aunt, we'll beat them," Oxy swung his arm in the air.

Elphy now commanded the team. "Pick up that thick rope, Chimp, and tie the two bigger logs together. We must put the bridge across the river as soon as possible… Oh my God! How *time flies*! Gurela, help him…. Come on guys, you can do it… Be fast."

Chimp and Gurela were the only ones who could use their fingers most efficiently.

"What about the third log, Uncle?" asked little Horsy.

"It's for Rhiny."

Rhiny was surprised to hear that, "For me, Elph? What the heaven shall I do with it?"

"I'll tell you," said Elphy, with a smile. "You have a big role to play." Then he turned to Chimp, "Have you tied the logs, Chimp?"

"Yes Elph… Now these logs can support three lions at a time."

"All right, then. Let's move ahead… hmmm… We'll set our bridge at that spot. Follow me." Elphy entered the river and stood at a spot in the middle of the flow. He felt no fear while doing so because he was too heavy to be flown away. Rhiny, Boary and other animals pushed the bridge over the river and Elphy placed the far end of the bridge between the two firm rocks.

Chimp was quite happy with the work they had done. "Perfect. No wave can take it away now."

"And what after the lions cross?" asked Boary.

"Just push it into the river. It will float away like grass."

"Awesome, children! Who could have thought we animals would construct a bridge one day? Really, *necessity is the mother of invention.*" Old Katy was overwhelmed with emotions. Tears rolled down her cheeks. No animal had ever built such a magnificent thing before. It was their teamwork that made this miracle possible.

Bobby wanted to make sure that lions cross the river, "Let's put some food near the other end of the bridge to lure the lions. And make it notably visible so that the lions can see it *right at first sight.*"

Animals searched for and found something at the riverside -- a dead old goat. Perhaps, it had drowned in the river and reached there with the flow. They placed it near the far end of the bridge.

They arranged it in such a manner that it looked *alive and well.* Meanwhile, Moly and team had widened the ditch. They filled it with river water to hide its shallowness. They covered its side facing the Wonder Forest with sharp thorns.

"Splendid!" said Elphy. "Now they won't dare jump over to the other side. And once we put the burning wood and cinders here, they won't come near this only passage to our island. Now I'll make the third log stand here… " And he did just that. "Monk, cover it with some vines and branches. It should look like a living tree. Rhiny, you will ram into our 'fake tree' when the lions are watching. They will get scared when they see an angry Rhino downing a tree," Elphy disclosed his plan.

"I'll growl *in full swing*. Let's not give them a chance to think that we are weak," added Bobby.

"Oh.. So you want to *play a bluff*, Uncle. Uncle Elphy and you are both *as tricky as monkeys*. Ooops… sorry Uncle Chimp!" and little Zebby smiled. Chimp smiled too, and winked at him. He loved children.

"We should keep them away *by hook or by crook*, kid," said Elphy.

Chimp gathered more wood for fire. By the night, they had gathered a large stock-pile near the pass. Now they were *ready for whatever may come.*

Olu was back with his '180-degree-rotatable' neck. He was assigned the task of *keeping an eye* on the lions at night. He informed them, "Lions are not far away. They are asleep right now. They will be here by tomorrow noon."

His information scared the kids. After all, children are children. Lions always scare them.

Bobby tried to cheer them up. "Don't worry, you little soldiers. *The darkest hour comes just before the dawn.* I wish we meet them tonight. I want to see their faces when we scare them away. Now tell me, who will put the burning stick on the wood?"

All the young ones forgot their fear and shouted "me…me…no, me… hey, I'm older than you…" and so on. And they gathered around Bobby.

"All right, all right. You all will… you all can.

But, not before you have a sound sleep. Tonight we'll all sleep here so that we can start our work with the first ray of the rising sun. Come on kids, it's story time.... Listen carefully. Once there was a big lion, the king of the jungle.....".

Bobby told them the story of a rabbit that had killed a lion by trick. The rabbit made the lion see his own reflection in a deep well, which the lion perceived to be another lion. He jumped into the well to fight him and killed himself.

"Why don't we just kill the lions?" little Deery asked curiously.

"Because we are good animals. We don't kill until forced to," replied Bobby.

"Then why do the lions kill?"

"Because it's their very nature. They see us as their food. But even they don't kill until they are hungry."

Elphy interrupted them, "Only the humans take more than they need. They kept me in a circus for months. Thank God, I was able to break free." There was bitterness in his voice.

Bobby showed him the positive side of it, "But Elph, you learnt something useful from them, like how to create and control a fire! Trust me, *God is great*. He never does anything without a purpose. *There is a reason for everything.* And we know that there are good human beings too. The ones who treat wounded animals and save dying ones. I'm sure they will all *get back on track* one day."

After a long, tiring day, they all went to sleep. Elders encircled the children for their protection. The forest grew quiet once again. Only Olu was *keeping a watch* over the jungle. In fact, Bobby, Katy and other elders were just pretending to be asleep. How could they sleep? They were worried. And they were praying.

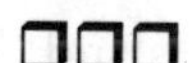

The Judgement Day

Finally, the *judgment day* arrived. All the animals were in full swing. They were eager to confront the scary predators. Parents had done everything they could to secure their shelters, *just in case* the lions manage to enter the island. They had instructed their children not to make the slightest noise. Lions must not get a hint about the presence of the kids.

Eggie reported that the lions were approaching. "Guys, they are almost *within a stone's throw*."

Chimp took two dry sticks and vigorously rubbed them together. Elphy had taught him the trick, and he had practised it again and again. Soon they were delighted to see a smoke.

"Now put some dry leaves and wood on it, Chimp," ordered Elphy. Chimp did as he was told. The fire was started. Then, they placed the burning sticks on the woodpile near the passage.

The fire could be seen even from a distance. Rhiny took his position near the 'fake tree'. Elphy and Bobby stood near the mouth of the passage. Chimp had collected big and small stones to throw at the lions. Gurela was doing push-ups. He was, as usual, angry and was shouting, "How dare the lions look at my territory....". Soon the lions appeared at a distance. Elphy trumpeted "Chiyaaaaaaaaaan....".

Lions got a bit scared when they heard it. One of them whispered, "An angry elephant! I don't like that." Still they moved on. They reached near the passage. Now they could see the two paths: the obstructed one leading to the island, and the other one, the bridge, to cross over to the other island. They were confused.

Lion 1, the eldest brother, wanted to collect others' opinions, "Which path should we take, brothers? On one, we have an angry elephant, on the other, a bridge over the river."

Lion 2 (the one with a broken leg) was much careless. "Can't you see the fire? Let's take the bridge. It looks safe. Seems as if God has constructed it for us."

"Fire is a matter of hours. I think we should stay. Small animals live near the elephants for protection. If we get them, we might have a party tonight," opined Lion 3.

Bobby got angry, and growled loudly "Grrrrrr… Grrrrrr… Grrrrrr…".

Lion 4 was a coward, "Even a bear! Sounds like a Himalayan bear. They are huge! I dare not challenge one."

Lion 5 was the strongest of them all. "So what? *Barking dogs seldom bite*. Bears are lazy. Let him hear this. AAGhrrrrrrrrrrrrrrrrrrrrrrr…" He roared so loudly that every animal could hear him.

The kids were now *terror-stricken*. This was the first time they had heard a lion. But Rhiny was all prepared. He knew that *actions speak louder than*

words. He came forward and smashed into the fake tree. The tree was down in one blow!

Lion 3 was now scared. "Did you see? He eradicated the tree with ONE SINGLE BLOW!"

Lion 5 was not convinced, "I think I can *smell a rat*. No rhino can do that. *Someone is cooking up something*. Why aren't these animals running away from fire? May be they are bluffing... they are trying *to throw dust in our eyes*. I'll take a chance." He wanted to jump over to the other side, but soon dropped the idea after seeing the thorns and cinders. *The grapes were sour to him*. "I think I'd like to wait a couple of hours." Then he shouted to scare them, "*You can't escape your destiny*!"

Now the lions were waiting at the passage. Bobby and Elphy were worried.

"I think fire won't keep them away for long. And what if it rains...? We should try something else too," suggested Bobby.

Chimp came up with a clever idea. "Hey, Monk! Where is the steel soccer you had stolen from men?"

Monk felt a bit embarrassed. "That was a long ago… when I was a naughty child. I'm using it as a water container these days."

"Go and get it. Hurry up!" shouted Chimp.

"What's so special about it? Men keep their food in it…"

"That's it!" explained Chimp. "Lions are scared of men. Once they have the slightest indication of presence of men on this island, they'll run away! Today your old soccer is *worth its weight in gold*."

Bobby fully agreed. "Rhiny has scared them. It's the time. *Strike while the iron is hot*."

Elphy praised Chimp. "What a *presence of mind*, Chimp."

Monk brought the soccer and handed it over to Chimp. Chimp started banging it against a rock "tann… tann… tann… tann…".

Lion 3 found this sound familiar. "You hear that? It's the noise of men's things… Oh, NO! The hunters are coming! May be they have started this fire to surround us. Oh God, we have been trapped!"

Lion 4 wanted no risk. "I won't stay here for another moment. I'm crossing the bridge.... Hey, look. There's a goat there! There can be so many of them..." And he headed straight for the bridge.

Lion 1 interrupted, "Wait! *All that glitters is not gold*, and all that looks scary is not so."

Lion 4 replied foolishly, "Well, who wants the gold when we have a goat...."

He ran towards the goat on the other side of the bridge. Other lions followed him, except lion 5. He was still suspicious. "But think what we can get here!"

Lion 1 replied calmly, "Brother! My experience says *a bird in hand is worth two in the bush*."

At last, lion 5 *gave in*. "I must reach there before they finish it."

"Elphy, Rhiny, now! Here comes *the golden opportunity*. Break the bridge," whispered Bobby.

Rhiny and Elphy pushed the bridge down into the river. All of a sudden, the lions heard many voices, "HURRAYYYYYY! We scared the lions away. YIPEEEEEEEEEEEE!"

Lion 5 shouted at his brothers, "I told you we were being fooled. See what we have lost! All the fortune *slipped through our fingers.*"

"*Never cry over the spilled milk,* brother. Let's move ahead. We will find some good food sooner or later. *Contentment is the greatest happiness,*" lectured Lion 1.

"*All stuff and nonsense. The more the merrier,* brother. You and your old mind. Huhhh....." yelled Lion 2.

And they walked away, frowning at each other.

The animals were now extremely happy. They were singing, dancing, playing and partying once again. They had won the greatest battle of their lives, perhaps.

Bobby reminded them, "I told you, *patience is a virtue.* This is a *red-letter day* for us. Let's celebrate the victory, friends. *All's well that ends well.*"

Now read the story once again. Remember, *Practice makes a man perfect.*

Meanings

- **Awe inspiring:** Breath taking; splendid
- **In the melting pot:** Likely to change
- **Give an ear:** To listen to someone
- **Seeing is believing:** You can believe what you see
- **Pride:** A group of lions
- **Misfortune never comes alone:** Many troubles come together
- **Scared stiff:** Extremely frightened
- **As soon as possible:** Without any delay; within the shortest time

- **Chicken-hearted:** Cowardly
- **Fight tooth and nail:** Make a strenuous effort using all the resources available
- **Empty vessels make the most noise:** The people with little knowledge usually talk the most
- **Lion's share:** The largest part of anything
- **To be honest:** To tell you the truth
- **Heart and soul:** Completely; enthusiastically
- **Born killers:** Natural predators (here)
- **Nip the danger in the bud:** Terminating the danger before it gets out of control
- **Win the horse or lose the saddle:** Everything at risk
- **A stitch in time saves nine:** A timely effort prevents more work later
- **In smooth waters:** Never in a trouble; Not worried about anything
- **Think before you speak:** One should think before he says something
- **To take by surprise:** To catch unaware

- **Light sleeper:** One who does not take a deep sleep
- **Bury the hatchet:** To forget about argument and disagreement
- **Dead serious:** Very serious
- **In a grave danger:** In a threatening situation
- **Might is right:** Superior strength dictates the terms
- **Kings can do no wrong:** One who rules doesn't admit his mistakes
- **Union is strength:** A group is more powerful than an individual
- **We shall sink or swim together:** We share a common fate
- **Sure shot:** Unfailing
- **Taking the bull by the horns:** To confront a problem openly
- **Castles in the air:** Plans that have very little chance of success
- **Head-on:** In open conflict
- **Fortune favours the brave:** Good luck comes to those who take risk

- **It takes two to quarrel:** A person does not quarrel against himself
- **Get back on track:** Resuming the correct course
- **A mare's nest:** A hoax or fraud
- **Arrive at a decision:** To make a decision
- **Coming events cast their shadows before:** Significant events are preceded by their signs
- **There is no smoke without fire:** There might be some reason behind what is happening
- **Bad blood:** Hate; Animosity
- **Win-win situation:** A situation in which every party wins
- **Help your luck, so that your luck helps you:** Help yourself
- **God helps those who help themselves:** One should not merely ask for divine help; But must work himself to get something
- **Leave no stone unturned:** Make every possible effort
- **Broke free:** Got free

- **Double-edged sword:** Something that has both a good and a bad side
- **Within a stone's throw:** At a short distance
- **Might and main:** With all the strength
- **Keep an eye on:** Watch someone carefully
- **Know which way the wind blows:** Note the changes taking place in the situation
- **Rest assured:** Be certain
- **In command:** Leader; Responsible for success of a team
- **Time and tide wait for none:** Time does not stop for anything to happen
- **Herculean task:** A difficult task
- **Child's play:** Easy task
- **Strong enough:** Sufficiently strong
- **Share the same opinion:** Have the same opinion
- **Life is precious:** Life must be preserved (here)
- **Tit for tat:** Repayment in kind
- **Bear the brunt:** To withstand the worst part of something

- **In no time:** In a very short time
- **A hard nut to crack:** A problem difficult to solve; A tough thing to do
- **No pleasure without pain:** Fruitful works are usually tough
- **If a job is worth doing, it is worth doing well:** When you do something; Do it well
- **Once and again:** Repeatedly
- **Dead on their feet:** Extremely tired
- **Call it a day:** Stop working
- **Going on:** Happening
- **So far:** Up to the present time
- **By all means:** Without fail
- **Size doesn't matter:** Skills are more important than one's size (here)
- **Every dog has its day:** Even a lowly person leads or enjoys in his best times
- **Having a tough time:** Passing through a tough or bad phase
- **Too few to make it in time:** Few in number to complete the task within set time limit

- **Figured that out:** Determined
- **Fool proof plan:** A very simple; Well-designed plan
- **Miss the target:** Don't succeed, fail
- **Make up for something:** To provide something good so that something bad seems less important
- **Cover up for someone:** To conceal someone's wrongdoing
- **Do the impossible:** Making something that looks impossible happening
- **To burn the candle at both ends:** To work extremely hard
- **There is no hard and fast way to success:** There is no shortcut to success
- **Mammoth task:** A huge task
- **Move the mountain:** Move a huge weight (referring to logs here)
- **Throw together:** Cause to associate, combine
- **In a body:** As a formal team or group
- **Out of breath:** Breathing with difficulty because of tiredness

- **Keep the things rolling:** Keep moving (here)
- **Dog tired:** Very tired
- **Putting the cart before the horse:** Doing the things in a wrong order
- **Second to none:** Ahead of others
- **Only the wearer knows where the shoe pinches:** Only the sufferer knows his pain
- **Much ado about nothing:** A big fuss over a trifle
- **Knock off:** Finish, complete
- **Went through:** Bore, suffered
- **Let sleeping dogs lie:** Let the inactive problems remain inactive
- **Hang about:** Spend time in a place; roam about
- **Find a weak spot:** Find a weakness
- **At sixes and sevens:** Confused
- **A black sheep:** A least reputable person
- **Plays fast and loose:** Very irresponsible
- **A man of word:** A person who keeps promises

- **Red handed:** While committing a crime
- **Staring us in the face:** We are facing; in front of us
- **Fly out:** Run away
- **Unanimous decision:** United decision; complete agreement
- **To tide over the crisis:** To get rid of the crisis
- **Ups and downs:** Good and bad times
- **Show fight:** Assume a fighting attitude; outbrave
- **Slow but sure:** Slow but unstoppable
- **In a while:** After a short time period
- **A friend in need is a friend indeed:** A friend in bad times is a real friend
- **The sooner, the better:** Should happen as early as possible (waiting eagerly for something to happen)
- **To blow own trumpet:** Praise oneself
- **Make it:** Complete the task
- **Burning the midnight oil:** Working for long hours

- **Contingency plan:** A plan for a possible emergency
- **Down to earth:** Realistic
- **God's will be done:** What God desires will happen
- **Hope for the best and prepare for the worst:** Have a positive attitude; Yet prepare for a possible crisis
- **Time flies:** Time passes quickly
- **Necessity is the mother of invention:** Inventions take place when we need something
- **Right at first sight:** Right when seen for the first time
- **Alive and well:** Living and healthy
- **In full swing:** Peak performance
- **Play a bluff:** To mislead someone; To trick
- **By hook or by crook:** Use any method to get the task done
- **Ready for whatever may come:** Ready for anything that could happen
- **The darkest hour comes just before**

the dawn: Worst phase comes just before improvement

- **There is a reason for everything:** Nothing happens without a cause
- **Keeping a watch:** To observe
- **Judgment day:** The day of final judgment
- **Barking dogs seldom bite:** One who makes threats seldom carries them out
- **Terror-stricken:** Filled with terror
- **Actions speak louder than words:** Doing has more significance than saying
- **Smell a rat:** Suspect that something is wrong, or there is a bluff
- **Someone is cooking up something:** Someone has a plan
- **To throw dust in eyes:** To mislead someone
- **The grapes are sour to him:** What he desires cannot be attained
- **You can't escape your destiny:** You will have your fate
- **Worth its weight in gold:** Very valuable

- **Strike while the iron is hot:** Take advantage of an opportunity
- **Presence of mind:** Ability to act rightly in any situation
- **Trapped:** Caught by a trick
- **All that glitters is not gold:** Something that attracts may or may not be valuable
- **A bird in the hand is worth two in the bush:** Better accept something than lose everything
- **Gave in:** Submitted
- **The golden opportunity:** An excellent opportunity
- **Beat off:** Drove away
- **Slipped through fingers:** Got out of grasp
- **Never cry over the spilled milk:** Don't cry for what has happened and cannot be changed
- **Contentment is the greatest happiness:** One should remain happy with whatever he has
- **Stuff and nonsense:** Makes no sense at all
- **The more the merrier:** More is always better

- **Red-letter day:** A very important day
- **Patience is a virtue:** Having patience is good
- **All's well that ends well:** An event is good if it has a good ending, no matter if something went wrong along the way